Beneath the Baobab

poems by

Amelia Blossom Pegram

Arable Press   Louisville, Kentucky

Beneath the Baobab

FIRST EDITION

Printed in the United States of America

ISBN 0-9723524-6-5

Arable Press
514 Washburn Avenue
Louisville KY 40222

arable@insightbb.com   www.arablepress.com

For

daughter—Melanie

my first Kentucky friend—Hazel

members of the Chartreuse Table

my sounding board—Tricia, Dorothy, Anne,
Kathleen, Joy, David, Joe.

TABLE OF CONTENTS

In Africa, In America   9

THE BAOBAB   11
A LETTER TO MY DAUGHTER   12
PRAISE SONG   13
THE ROCK   14
AIDS EPIDEMIC   15
BON VOYAGE   16
ARRIVAL   18
HARVEST   19
DRUM CALL   20
THE GRIOT   21
MISSIONARY   22
ABDUCTION   24
EULOGY   26
REWARD   28
WHAT SHALL I TELL THE CHILDREN   30
LIBERATION   32
QUIERO   33
LOSS   34
THE COMMISSION   36
MIGRATION 2003   38

The Art of Movement   39

STRANGE FRUIT	41
BIRDS AT SUNRISE	42
SATHIMA'S ANCESTRAL CRY	43
INVITATION TO THE DANCE	44
ON THE TIDE	45
UPRIGHT	46
WORDS	47
GUITAR	48
THE OCEAN	49
JAZZ IN CENTRAL PARK	50
NETTED	52
NIGHT MUSIC	53
LORD OF THE DANCE	54
ON LINE	56
ENCOUNTER	57
NEEDS	58
AUDITION	59
WEDNESDAY AT JACK FRY'S	60
QUESTIONS	62
IMAGES	63
LINEAR ALGEBRA	64
RECOLLECTION	66
OPUS	67
ON BROADWAY	68
PRAISESONG FOR THE MENTOR	69
SONG SOLITUDE	70
DANCING	71
ANTHOLOGY	72

Family   73

MARKERS   75
ABSENT   76
AFTER PICKING   78
BACK IN THE SADDLE   79
GIVE US THIS DAY   80
LETTER   81
MANGO   82
COPING   83
PRESENCE   84
HOMECOMING   85
SEGMENTS   86
BROKEN   87
CIRCLES   88
THE FIELD   90
THE TIP   91
FRIENDSHIP   92
REKINDLING   94
SEASON'S END   95
THE LANGUAGE OF LIFE   96
THE WALL   98
EVENING AT FISH EAGLE   100

ACKNOWLEDGMENTS

Thanks to the editors of the following periodicals, anthologies, and books in which some of these poems appeared previous to the publication of this book.

Moving Beyond Boundries: International Dimensions of Black Women's Writings, Vol. 1 1988
"Declaration"
"Quiero"

Thinker Review, 1992
"Segments"

Arable: A Literary Journal, Vol. 1 No. 1
"Guitar"
"Images"

Arable: A Literary Journal, Vol. 1 No. 2
"Upright"

Yellow Moon, # 17, 2005
"At Fish Eagle Lodge"

Voices of South Africa, Midfest Int'l Foundation, 1999
"The Commission"

"Segments" was reprinted in Amelia Blossom Pegram's second collection of poems, *Echoes Across a Thousand Hills*, Africa World Press, 1996.

In Africa, In America

THE BAOBAB

In this hot, dry, dusty season
you stretch your gnarled, black limbs
across the reddening sky
marking your place in the sunset.

Some of the old villagers
will not go near you now,
as they watch your branches
they see black mambas writhe
their shiny bodies in the evening breeze.

As I rest against your strong body
I see only your arms
moving slowly to the throb of the distant drum
and feel the comfort of the beat
reminding me of the sustenance you gather
from the depths of our land.

A LETTER TO MY DAUGHTER
for Melanie

Sometimes I see you
calmly gather your thoughts
concentrate
focus.
And know I cannot
reach inside your mind.
I am excluded.
You flex your muscles
and explode to action
with jaw taut
screaming silently
tossing sarcasm
against my molding.
We clash force against force,
Your body, mind and will
seeking self-direction.
I want only to shield
you from the pain of
traps I can foresee,
help you avoid
the briars of my growing years.
In these stormy times,
we shout our feelings,
when all we need
is to concentrate,
calmly focus
on our unconditional love,
strength of our bonds.

PRAISE SONG

for Leah Tutu

Leah,
wife, mother, equal partner,
did not walk in the shadow,
but rather side by side
with other leaders
in the struggle
for the rights of all oppressed.

With the tenacity of a lioness
she gathered domestic workers
into a strong band,
a union of women
to sustain their pride.

She fiercely decried
tourists ferried in coaches
to view township homes
and people,
like observing animals
in zoo cages.

Graceful Leah stood steel firm
against the evil apartheid laws
that imposed work choices
of scrubbing floors
washing and ironing
child minding for white madams.

With a warm and ready smile
she continues to walk in grace
teaching tolerance and forgiveness
in the now liberated South Africa.

THE ROCK
(Kalk Bay, South Africa 2004)

On this sizzling December day,
I sit on Jack Knife,
the rock midway
from shore to pier.
I recall my determination
to be a big kid
swimming out to this spot
away from the kindergartners.

On this rock memories
of adventure and safety
lap through my mind
with the harmony of gentle
warm Indian Ocean waves
moving over my legs
with rhythmic ebb and flow.

AIDS EPIDEMIC

Like a forest fire out of control
it rages across all borders.
Oak-strong men shrivel
as they wait.

No aid comes.

Women peer from eyes
sunken deep as wells
in the dry earth.

They wait.

Children no longer skip and sing
songs of joyous stories,
teasing family and friends.
Their laughter, like the summer rain,
does not come.

In this land, old customs to celebrate life
with singing, dancing and feasting
at each death,
have disappeared in pain
beyond crying.

There is no aid coming,
no profit to be made
by halting this fire scorching all in its path.

Men, women and children wait.

BON VOYAGE

Through airless summers
frigid winters
people packed
in decaying projects
survive in huddled spaces
tediously riding the tides
with roach-and-rat
creaking boards.
Mothers pacify infants
on shriveled breast.
Toddlers share play corners
with growing garbage.
Youth hang out in
gangways
where they are left to rot
or are fed to sharks
trading guns and drugs.
Easy money.
In this middle passage
the rickety vessel
transports
its cargo
to concrete plantations.
Factories and mills
afford space at the belt
work pieced to assembly.
In stuffy sweat shops
abductees cower under
overseers

whose tongues whip
threats
urge machines to
endless whirring.
From crumbling tenements
they come
to slave on cotton
fashioned
to corporate profits.
On these plantations
the slaves have no
patch
to grow their own
or time
to ham
the bones in
remembered rhythms.

At night they crawl
back to their berths
on crowded
ships
plying
trade
in human
suffering.

ARRIVAL

Through the morning mist
the mountain looms blue
across the bay.
After three months on the Indian Ocean
passengers are eager
to regain land legs.
Nazia and Abdurahman,
like Jonah, were spewed
from the belly of the vessel
on to the beach of "Bloubergstrand."
Far from their Malaya island home
and trades,
they are forced under guard
to build crude wood and leaves shelter.
The sandy beach marks the foundation
of a new existence—
sentence for political protest
against Dutch occupation.

HARVEST

A way never showed
a path we traveled
together
where we gathered
mushrooms, buttercups,
or picked
wild strawberries.
It was always
the going, the parting
you wanted to rehearse,
when I welcomed
each beginning.

Now I have learned
to enter the ancient forest
unafraid,
alone in the joy
of the gathering.

DRUM CALL

for Earbie Johnson

Like the ripples
from a single stone
your drum-spirit
moves in ever-widening
circles
to encompass and move
to rhythm and song
young and old.
Through your hands
the ancient voices speak
fast pounding
victory
slow swaying
serenity.
From the depth
of the drum
you scatter sounds
into kaleidoscopic patterns,
catching poems into dances
learned through the
blood of our ancestors.

THE GRIOT

If I could go back,
I would not hurry Ouma Jet
through any stories,
even those I had heard
over and over again.

I would not wonder how any face
could have that many wrinkles.
I would accept her explanation
that each line was an experience.
She said the deeper lines
were rivers of sorrow,
the wars that took her family,
Anglo-Boer, World I and II.

If I could return
I would not let her digressions
into all the family histories,
irritate.

But would wait
patiently
for Ouma Jet to say
"And now I'll go on with my story."

MISSIONARY

In his corner of Africa,
during the long drought
the fire could not feed
on the ecru grass
that disappeared into the cracked
mud.
In this hell
they light the ebony night
with wax and kerosene.
After their scrounged meal
they sleep spoon-nested
for shared warmth.

After the rains come
to this place,
as always
the only running water
courses over the sharp rocks
grinding to silt of the delta.

The drought-stilled drums
again throb praise-songs.
Dancers gather at the water
in thanks
for panther-black skins
not uncleansed by the
ghost-maker.

To this corner of Africa

you came
with your medicine bag
for the disappeared.
You of the many tongues
who never learned to speak
their language.
You of the strange music,
sounds whining out of
pipes you press with black
and white.
Music your god required
in his praise.
You who scorned the drums,
Kora, mbira, and shakerey.
The "been-to" sons and daughters
shake their heads
when you say they need
no switches for light,
no faucets and irrigation,
no toilets to flush.

The been-to children
spit on the ground,
stomp on your grave,
say the chant of truth.
"You needed this hell
unchanged
so you can be sure
by your big deeds
to reach your god
in your heaven."

ABDUCTION

If I find a metaphor,
My Sister,
to wrap around
your pain
snatched by your hair
into their white car,
would the slashing of
your breast
the sodomy by
tree limb
behind the Kroger store
seem not quite
so heinous?
Should I pretty up
with words
your crawling to the
sidewalk?
Can I disregard
the warnings
of your two white attackers
to give the same
to all Nigger bitches?

I am not inclined
to veil my anger
in figurative language.

Kidnap
Rape

Sodomy
Slashing
stand
naked.

Naked as you left my sister
on the Middle Passage
snatched from
her native African soil.

Raped
in the cotton fields
her blood
mixed into the clay
of Georgia
her black skin peeled
into the Mississippi earth.

Now kidnapped
after a hard day's work
from the bus-stop
at 28th and Broadway
I see you, My Sister,
carrying memory.

I see rising out
of rekindled
cross burnings
the brazen return
of the now uncloaked
night-riders.

EULOGY

The old people said,
"It is your duty.
If you can't mourn
for your husband,
hire those who will."
Having spent all her tears
in their marriage,
she hired official mourners
to send him out of this world,
though she could not,
no matter how many tears
were shed,
assure
he would land
in a desirable place.

On the chilly April morning
they gathered around the grave
in the moth-soft mist.
The black-veiled cemetery women
sang, shouted and wailed loud
to earn their payment.

The minister roared
as if wanting the mist
to turn to torrents.

He warmed up to his
praises as the sobbing grew.

"Cyril was a good man.
He worked hard.
He cared for his family.
His lovely wife, Maria, here
and these five beautiful children.
They never wanted for anything.
Cyril worked overtime most nights.
I often met him on the street
late at night, coming home from work."

He took a deep breath.
Got up his second wind.
The pause brought
"Amens," "Hallelujahs,"
the "Yes, Jesus" choruses,
the minister wanted.

Before he could launch
his next phase of eloquence,
Maria gathered her children.
"We're at the wrong place.
Your father is not being buried here, today."

REWARD

He steps out of his home,
a cave on the slopes of Table Mountain,
dressed to kill,
in gray plus-fours
black high-collared frock-coat,
white lace fronted shirt,
high-crowned, wide-brimmed
dark brown, felt hat.
The boots with no laces
denotes his slave status.

When Hannie's boots
clop on the cobble street
of the Malay Quarters,
jeers and spitting
erupts
in the usual quiet
of Friday afternoon prayers.

The men sit in groups
discussing the Imam's message.

Women gather to talk
family
as they pound the spices
with pestle in mortar.

Hannie cannot avoid
the street, which like a main artery

goes to the heart
of the town.

Crowds have gathered
on the square
for another festival and spectacle.

Hannie walks with all the pride
he can puff into each step,
swinging the noose
in his right hand
tightly holding the end of the rope
in his left.

In the Malay Quarters
all will be at evening prayers
when he returns
up the cobble stones
with his reward –
a long black braid.

WHAT SHALL I TELL THE CHILDREN?

for the memory of Ken Saro-Wiwa (hanged in
Nigeria for speaking out against Exxon)

For more than twenty-five years
the poets sang sad songs
of Exxon spills
crops failing
fish dying
people starving
their villages burned
rhymeless.
His strength gathered families
against well-greased pollution
that slipped his people
below Shell's profits
pumped from their soil.
The bard wove his words
in cord patterns of songs
fabric of revolt.

Now what shall I tell the children
of the five-timed-tried looped rope
that cut off his life
by General order?

Shall I tell them
his voice cannot be silenced?
Like a tree dormant
in the winter of this season
his ideas remembered

in his last breath
"May God take my soul.
The struggle continues."
His hope
will be revived
into voiced green words
of a new season.

LIBERATION

F
R
E
E
D
O
M
three
hundred
fifty
unfranchised
years
long coming
to sardined townships
where children treasure-hunt
in dungheaps,
grandmothers patch peopled pants.
FREEDOM
slow coming
sacrificed for
in poverty
beaten down to menial jobs
cupped hands receiving
wages from sneering pockets
liberation
painfully coming
through splintered dreams
of humanity
warrior red sunsets.
FREEDOM
should be BIG.

QUIERO

I want to stretch my body
on your rolling undulations
inhale your smells
fresh pine, heather
feel your breath on my face
bare arms, legs,
let your substance drip
through my fingers.
I long to be with you
in springtime
when fresh green grass
and daisies white, yellow,
paint Table Mountain,
when the sea breeze floats
salty damp warmth
fanning me
as I burrow my body
comfortably into your
contours,
let your rich earth
fall through my fingers
squooze between my toes.
I yearn to be home.

LOSS

In celebration of a new day dawning,
she stretched her arms
to reach the sky
raised her face
to greet the sun,
twirled her dandelion seed dance.
In joyous ritual she delighted
in comfort of familiar rhythm.

Clanging cymbals
Explosion
Destruction
Innocence destroyed.

She crumbles to the ground
numbed by the violent
invasion of her body
knows not how to rid
this evil now within.

Water showered down in torrents
cannot cleanse her body
dirt-caked to her very soul.

No drums beat
familiar rhythms
to recapture dances
of abandon.

Her soft moans and sobbing
turn to shouts of vengeance now.
She wants to hunt the rapist
tear him limb from limb.
Dance her victory upon his very soul.

Will she ever celebrate
another dawning, arms outstretched
in a morning's ritual dance?

THE COMMISSION
for Bishop Desmond Tutu and his historic contributions

I cannot bring the words past the heart
in song.
Nor beat a drum
on my chest,
when I recall
monster begat
from a long line
or reforming itself
in history and myth.
If Grendel ravished maidens
or the Inquisitors
hounded "heretics,"
or Hitler strutted
his Aryan supremacy
across the ashes of "the other,"
or Amin destroyed his own,
and the tales repeat
in a monotony to dull
the human spirit,
then I cannot sing.
I can only moan
or wail for my
mothers, fathers, brothers, and sisters,
devoured by the Apartheid Monster.
The monster who tore
family from family,
displaced neighborhoods
and slaughtered

with impunity.
Apartheid was his name.
Name of terror.
He tortured, imprisoned
and with demonic mirth
struck death blows.
So how can I sing?
I can sing the praise of my sisters
Helen, Lilian, Dulcie, Ruth
and more.
My brothers Steve and Neil
hear my silent songs.
But for the monster no drum beats.
I will ring the bell
of warning.
As Truth and Reconciliation
look the beast in the eye,
the bell will warn for vigilance
that the monster be
delimbed,
not be allowed to have
blood coursing through
new tentacles.
If I can be assured of
his total demise
I can change my moans,
call my heart to join
the drum beats
and sing my songs
of thanksgiving.
Shout my words of praise.

MIGRATION 2003

The unsuspecting slender bill curlews
flapping frantically glide softly
showing warm cinnamon wing linings,
now travel in wedge-shaped flocks
from Africa to the Tigris,
their resting place.
There they always sing joyous cur-lee melodies
in celebration of return to nesting.

On the journey across the sky
the marbled teals muster
in small compact groups,
singing in flight
on the 7,000 mile migration
to stop at the Euphrates
their ancient renewal spots.

The voiceless white storks
stretch black and white necks
red beaks and legs
as they soar in unsynchronized disorder
to reach the loud bill-clappings
of reunion rituals along eternal Iraqi marshes.

In this March and April
these birds cannot know
their million flaps and songs
of annual spring migration
to northern breeding grounds
will be shattered by stronger stealth fliers –
black hawks, blue tails, super hornets, silver eagles.

The Art of Movement

STRANGE FRUIT

Billie Holiday sang
of the strange fruit
ripe and rotting
on southern trees.

They could not have been
sweet orange rind kumquats
bitter sour yellow flesh
trickling tickling juice.

Nor could they have been
smooth pink or white fleshed guavas
brimful with crunchy pits,
from a tree whose leaves,
the old folks say,
brewed an arthritis cure.

Nor the dense gritty fleshed quinces
a day's acidic chew
growing on hedge-rows
like their relatives, the rose bushes.

Certainly not the papayas
ripening yellow on tall palms
fruit giving juicy salmon-pink flesh.

Billie Holiday's fruit
stretched forcibly tall
dangled from lower limbs
black flesh oozing red.

BIRDS AT SUNRISE

Like the magician
releasing the white bird
from his hands,
she set the dove
free across her canvas
with strokes passing
fleetingly through my vision.
Then she sent
a flock rising
to greet the lilac dawning,
while I still wonder
what motion released the first.

SATHIMA'S ANCESTRAL CRY

for Sathima Bea Benjamin

deep low
moan
wail through
high
primal scream
from first
birth
mixed with
joy rhythms
to blend
in the music
changes of
life experience
through labor
and birth
pain
the woman
from
the beginning
of time
brought forth
blues into jazz.

INVITATION TO THE DANCE

Your music wraps
around
in warm secure
chords
binding me
in quick-step melody
in the strong thrusts
of major beats
key to the dance.

We roll in rhythmic flow
bodies glow
in the tango's
passion
winding us
down
into satisfied
closeness of
the slow-dance.

We hold on
silently
through the
final waltz.

ON THE TIDE

We could laugh with abandon
at the toe-tickling water
of the ebbing tide,
race with the wind
across the beach,
collapse in child-like giggly heaps,
savor the honesty of our love.

The receding water gave us
vast stretches
for treasure hunts
where the sand-dollar was prized
even above the starfish.
I was not drawn by the rarity
of the shells
only the colors and shapes.

My collection is carefully boxed
with memories
fond even if tinged with bitterness.

I never knew if you swam out
with the tide
or climbed to drier ground
when the flow threatened.

I was absorbed in the movement
of the hermit crab
then found myself alone.

UPRIGHT

for bassist, Buster Williams

Signaling his deep knowledge
of the dance they have made their own,
he pulls her shiny, brown curves
close,
wraps his arms around her ample body,
rests her neck on his shoulder.

With right index and middle fingers
he sets the rhythm
at the base of her spine,
left hand running string to string
evokes tune variations.
Fingers work in harmony
drawing powerful vibrations deep within.

His face reflects the pain and pleasure
the ecstasy
of the music they explode
across the audience.

WORDS

You have forgotten
the joy we shared
in the sounds of words
we created.
The sounds we used for dancing,
skipping through our new languages
in the cool of the setting sun.
We wrung melodies from new words,
cherished the old ones.

You once knew how to make
your letters sing
and I remembered our dances
with words.

Now, in your academic grandeur,
you have learned only
to strip all words
to dry bones
that can't even rattle a tune.

GUITAR

With ear low over the guitar
he moves caressingly
from chord to chord
strumming the tunes
blues moaning
deep out of
the pain settled
below the heart.
He draws the cries
of long suffering
with twangs
wailing strings
plucked.
And then to break
through the melancholy
he ups the tempo
building to frenzied strum
underscored with beats
pounded in the side.

THE OCEAN

Even when you are
shrouded
in dark, gray
blusters
flinging white caps
on dull sand and
massive boulders,
I am awed into
staying in your
power.
I sit transfixed
on the deserted pier,
recalling the golden
ripples of your
sun-kissed body,
when you gently caressed
my ankle,
then drew me further
into your trust,
softly wrapping around
my thighs, breasts, shoulders
your womb-warmth.
Like a gigolo
you showed complete
charm and attention.
I never thought to guard
against your undertows.
Even when unbalanced by
your treachery
I remain enchanted.

JAZZ IN CENTRAL PARK

Mid-afternoon heat ushers listeners
to shaded side seats
and picnic set-ups under trees.
Musicians sweat through
canopied performances.
Children drip across grass
after running through pool and fountain.
The woman in bright yellow
with golden dred-locks
sways to the blues
swings with the big beat
jumps ovations.
She waves her own-rolled in left
brown-jugged libation in right.

A saxophone player steps up for a solo.
"Let's hear some Trane
C O L T R A N E
I mean, The Trane." She shouts.
Ululates approval.
Gets her brown jug refilled,
settles back for deep drags.
By early evening
she struts a measured sway
from vendor to vendor,
haggling in the African market-place.

The music draws her back
to the front-row lawn chairs.

Gentle ballads do not move her to applause.
Local artists are encouraged by her renaming.
"Speak to me Rufus. Work them strings, Reid."
She urges the bassist to stretch his solo.
The drummer becomes Max Roach.
The pianist brings her to her feet
in praise of The Duke.
Her enthusiasm spreads from row to row
as the music reaches out
in comfortable waves through the park.

Cicadas, frogs, and dogs chorus in mixed keys.

The vocalist swings into
"Bye-bye Blackbird" with a loud response
from roosting blackbirds.

The golden-dreded woman
mellows to deep strums
as warm darkness enfolds.

NETTED

With the warm water
gently lapping around my ankles
we gathered shells, starfish,
and pebbles.
You taught me
to pry mussels
scrub them clean
for our picnic.
When the moonlight and fire
danced shadows,
you would not let me explore
beyond the two rocks,
sentinels to our cove.
If only I could venture
from your closeness
I knew if allowed
into the breakwater –
breathe deep
pull hard
stroke by stroke
spurt
through wave over wave –
I would surely
swim to the
center of the setting sun
reach out to touch
the sky at its meeting
with the sea.

NIGHT MUSIC

The song lilting through my head
night after night,
is not one you ever sang,
whistled or even hummed.
Your work pulsed with an earthy dance beat,
strong percussions,
not the waltz of hills alive.
I did not invite Julie Andrews
to perform in my head.
I'd rather stomp a rhythm with Aretha,
recall how the beat vibrated in our dancing
all night long.
I want to hear your chocolate baritone
caress me
live across the hills.

LORD OF THE DANCE

I keep a steady beat
in this old oak rocking chair
'cause God got rhythm.

Watch the seasons
come and go in perfect
four- four time.
If you can't dance to that,
try the waltz of the tides,
flow ebb, flow ebb.
Sure God's got rhythm.

I danced with Him
spinning across the earth
autumn leaves spiraling
quicker and quicker,
laughing, laughing,
till I was dizzy.
Any dance you can name
He can do.
From the stiff minuet
of the stately bending branches,
to the hora, samba, kwela,
or the high-stepping, fast-kicking,
skirt-twisting white-capped waves
in the can-can,
to the slow moving swaying
through corn.
And you should have seen

Him tango with me
on the hilltop
and dip me with
the setting sun.
Yea, yea,
God sure got it.

ON LINE

When I was made to believe
the King James Bible
was absolute
the words were the literal
truth
Gospel not to be refuted
even by syllable,
I had a hard time
with God's book
of Accounting.
It was the same
problem I had with Santa.
Just how big was the
Book of Deeds?
And how many trees
were sacrificed in the making?
Now I am told I need
not worry
about the trees used,
or the space
the books take up.
Both God and Santa
can be reached
@AOL.COM

ENCOUNTER

I pulled my shoulders back,
stepped high
as your whistle put a lilt in my step.

I chuckled,
heard yours in response.

I glanced around,
found you, bird
mocking me.

NEEDS

If I had known your needs,
I could have shaped my wants
beyond the comfort of a crackling fire
chuckling up the sooty chimney
as the snow held its silence
piled against the door.

I could have foregone the joy
of our walks to the top of the hill
to listen to the lark at sunset
high against the peach-skin sky.

Perhaps I did not want to see,
your need to let me hear
the hollow ring in your laughter
as you petal-plucked love-me and love-me-nots
making it always come to love-me.

I wanted only the softness of the silence
to cover all the scars of living
and did not know you needed
to be the fire
flinging sparks
to scorch your brand
upon my soul.

AUDITION

His bright red coat glistened
in the early morning sunshine,
the light spot-on.
He knew he was the handsomest
bird on the line,
the starring role assured.
The others trying to make it
would be ignored.
He sat quietly showing
his best side,
while the rest
did their song and dance.
They had selected to be
in her face
as they performed on the fallen branches
below which she watched and listened.
In the keen competition
for the lead role,
they forgot the basic eye-contact rule,
did not see her quietly slip out.
He watched and was in full flight
for the nailing of the part.
The others left without the producer
they auditioned for.

WEDNESDAY AT JACK FRY'S
for Ray Johnson

Before nine o'clock, loud laughter erupts
from this table, booth, or that.
Voices intermingle across the room
deafening the solitary
perched-on-barstool customer.
Over the hum of well-fed diners
wined to raucous conversations
the music enters,
settles to a place, deep comfort.

Ray's piano grounds
rhythms in countless variations
tune after tune.
Scotty's horn joins,
weaves with piano
lifts to new pitch solo.
The thin applause from the customer
at the bar
cuts through the dinner cacophony.

After nine o'clock,
conversations settle
into boothed whispers.
Laughter bursts
like soft bubbles.

A suave silver-gray man
woos a willowy blonde

with full-bodied red wine,
chateaubriand,
wadded tip for players of
unforgettable sentimental requests
to waft from piano and horns
folding into familiar jazz standards.

Ray sharpens the air
with original compositions,
leading Scotty's horns in improvisation
to patterned overlays
in lyrical excitement
warming to applause.

The air stills at evening's end.

QUESTIONS

1

Could roses flying
from tree to tree
be cardinals perched
on thorned stems?

2

If
too much sweet bird song
irritates
as heavy perfume
cloys,
will too much love
oppress?

3

How could a strong
hard working
swift walking
mother
wither to wren frailty?

IMAGES

Time was,
black velvet conjured
opulence
deep
soft
living
black-tie elegance.

Now the plush fabric
evokes
Elvis Presley
hip gyrating
Jail House Rock
slow dancing
Love Me Tender
at every flea market.

LINEAR ALGEBRA

I could never understand
why I needed to know
when a train leaving at 9 a.m.
then traveling at 60 m.p.h
would pass a train from the opposite direction
leaving at 8 a.m. at 70 m.p.h.
I only wanted to know
what time I would get where I was going.
Who or what passed, was of no importance.

Perhaps the engineer or line-switcher
needed to know.
I had heard tell of terrible stories
when the lines were not switched
at the right time.

I told the teacher I didn't see the point
when I never could get the correct answer.
Got sent to detention with my smart-alecky mouth.

My father suggested it was to help
in awareness of surroundings.
Knowing who we passed on our journey
was important, he said.

But I think he got mixed-up
with the other warning
about knowing who you passed on the way up
because of having to come down.

I think there was also something
About being helped on the way up.

In that train which left at 9 a.m
and traveled at 60 m.p.h
I knew I could, if I cared, check my watch
when I saw the other passing.

RECOLLECTION

In the long of winter
nights stretched in front of the fire
we conjured stories
about the characters in the flames,
the delicate creatures
who were always chased
by the ogres
that lurked in the coals
then sprang from their hiding places
in the glowing embers.

The dancers lifted to new life
were cheered by us
as we watched their escape.

The monsters' fiery red eyes
no longer scared us
as we swept them out
next morning
in the ashes.

OPUS

She did not want
the single violin
of the one star movie
with which he was content.
She wanted all the strings
even the whole orchestra.
Woodwinds swelling,
brass resounding calls
to full percussion,
kettle drums booming
to the final cymbal clashes
crescendos
fade in gentle diminuendo.

ON BROADWAY

On the corner of 1st and Broadway
he leaned painfully on his crutches,
left knee tight against chest
right hand held firm
to his crutch
and to peak of alms cap.

In a deep baritone, he sang a plaintive blues song,
nodded appreciation for each contribution.

Between songs he kept a steady patter:
his war history,
injuries graphically described,
need for help,
government neglect.

I was touched.
Added my dollar.

At five o'clock, the cross-town bus appeared.

He stuffed his take into his pockets,
donned his cap,
threw his crutches behind the plant stands.
Sprinted across the street to the bus.

PRAISESONG TO THE MENTOR

in memory of Leon Driskell

You taught me to hold
words warm in my hands,
pass them over my palms.
You showed me how to roll
each vowel, consonant, syllable,
across my tongue,
savor the tart, bitter, sweet.
Breathe in the full aroma.
In your memory
I release
the words
on the four winds
to dance in rhythms
fast and slow,
skip over the ground,
twist in the wind,
soar to touch the sky.
You gather my scatterings
return them fondly
for me to create
new patterns.
I return a toast
in full-bodied libation.

SONG SOLITUDE

When the need
to get away from the noise
of incessant bass drums
booming in the memory
overwhelms,
go to where wild creatures
are at peace.

In the Meditation Garden,
overlooking Big Meadow,
sitting,
the mind a clean sheet
on which to capture
images of all sounds,

sort out gentle nuances
in the seeming monotony
of subtle insect songs.

Then walk slowly around the lake
not disturbing the stillness
of the water.

Carry deep inside
the quiet freedom
of the space,
where wild creatures
are at peace.

DANCING

Balanced on stiletto heels
I was able to glide with you
in a waltz,
go with the rhythm of the foxtrot,
even dip in the tango.
My chiffon-layered skirt
swirled around me in the samba.
I knew we were the center
of the universe as I mastered
the required lean-back,
your hand firm at the base of my spine,
made the obligatory fixed smile
come natural.
We never missed a step
with every changing dance craze.

In my now sensible shoes,
I do well to sway to a gentle beat.

ANTHOLOGY

Between your covers
I discovered rhythm:
tides ebbing
gentle withdrawal
patterning the shore,
then rising
in flowing
white-capped waves
crashing on
stretched out beaches.

Between your covers
I discovered songs:
many voices
choirs of sirens
echoing across waves
from granite black rocks
washed
in breaking foam.

Between your covers
I discovered pain:
unbalancing courses
well-planned
hitting a sudden storm
rolling
struggling
to shore.

Family

MARKERS

We traveled year after year
counting milestones
to unplanned destinations.

We lingered on walks
along country roads
sitting on stone markers
planning our lives
like well-ordered maps.

We knew the easiest roads
for every season
but often dared the treacherous.

Now I recall each journey
sitting on this stone—
marker of your life.

ABSENT

He stands at the corner
bus-stop
oblivious of the wind
taking a short-cut
through his body.
His eyes glaze
into the fog he inhabits.
This fifteen-year old
disembodied from
community
family
self
does not acknowledge
the man and old woman
in the space.
"You should be at school, child.
We need all our young men
whole."
He makes no response
to the neighborhood grandma.
"You waste your time on him, Ma'am.
This boy long gone.
Ain't nobody home."
The boy turns up his jacket collar.
Crawls in deeper.
"Nobody home?" the old lady muses.
"Perhaps his doorbell doesn't work.
He doesn't hear the knocking.
What if somebody just opens the door.

Call out. We here. Hello."
The grandma puts a hand
on his arm.

The boy shivers.

AFTER PICKING

I pass my fingers
over the firm roundness
smooth and shiny
held in the palm of my hand.
I pull the skin
strip by strip
reveal rich red flesh.
I suck the sweet juice
let it drip slowly
down my throat
spill through my lips.
I roll the firm white seeds
of the pomegranate
between my teeth
savor all it offers.

BACK IN THE SADDLE

It's been so long.
She didn't remember how.

Swing leg over.
Position thighs close
around long banana saddle.
Back straight.
Shoulders slightly bent
with outstretched arms
to hold on tight.
Pump legs on pedals.

Riding a bike, nothing to it.

But she had never learned to ride

GIVE US THIS DAY

Dormant flour, salt, water,
await the yeast
to bring to rising
the bread we need.
We mix the yeast
with tepid water
and teaspoon of sugar
to start the bubbling.
Then pour into the well
we made in the flour
and salt.
We mix with spoonfolds,
then knead
with forceful fists,
each taking turns,
to pummel, slap, fold,
to shiny mass.
Well greased pans
accept the dough
for swelling,
then baking
slowly to golden brown.
The aroma assures
we will not need
today.

LETTER

All I had bottled
to tell you
over the years
I wrote in that letter.

Now there is nothing
I can say.

It was returned unopened
stamped
Deceased.

MANGO

I slowly peel
strip by strip
then pull flesh and skin
between my teeth
to let the juice come
thick and sweet
into my mouth,
ooze down my chin
a rich yellow nectar.
Stringy fibers catch
between my teeth
as I scrape the hard core
to whiteness.

COPING

If on this moonless surly winter night
I find no comfort in remembered love
I dare not loudly curse the bright starlight
For I now take no solace from above.
When from our marriage bed your warmth has passed
And I have only memories to hold
I will not lift my spirits from the vast
Enveloping darkness which my joy turns cold.
Although I wish to soar above this gloom
I cannot stir my soul to race with hope
For my love for you will now forever loom
And leave me in the dreariness to grope.
Despite murky clouds I'll harbor no spite
Though you in new love find such great delight.

PRESENCE

for Horace Bond

You never said you'd choose a bird.
But if you had,
it would've been
a long-winged petrel gliding across the ocean,
a kestrel soaring above castles in Europe
you always read about,
or even a great golden eagle
to claim all of America
your country.
You would've swooped down
for the dramatic entrance,
always your style.

I would've stood in awe.

Today you refuse to move
even as my car approaches.
I have to stop.
Walk down the drive.

How could I not recognize
the usual tilted head,
mischief in the stare
the twinkling eye laughing
at my surprise?

I stand in awe.

You never mentioned a robin.

HOMECOMING

She sat on her front porch
waiting for somebody to be first
to enter the empty house.
She saw the rooms
welcomeless
even if she liked to sink
into her father's favorite chair.
The setting was the coldness
she now gets from a television
not in color.
She wanted the warm brown
of her father's voice
to rumble through the rooms,
echo off the ceilings.
She waited out front
knowing she could not open a door
without then shouting her cheery hello.

SEGMENTS

If I need an "as" or a "like"
to shape a poem
of our marriage
let it be a grapefruit.
After I have discarded
the bitter rind
of my anger and regret
I bite into
the memories meat
bitter sour sweet
our flesh on the
bones of our daughter
your smile in her eyes
of brighter times
sour the juice
trickling with the
sucking of each segment
of our marriage
bitter
your inability to
slake your lust
on the grapefruit.

BROKEN

She intones teach me to pray
"Thy will be done"
even as she hurls
curses in that overcast valley.
She shafts anger
against her affliction
wondering why she was selected
for that descent.
There she prays to see
God's mercy in rays of light
slowly peeking through the mist.
She sees the hands of friends
wanting to guide her
to higher ground,
but she can not trust.
She wants no pity in words
or quiet embraces.
In that valley
she needs to throw stones
against the echoes
of her angry cries.

CIRCLES

I see her standing at the pawnshop
rubbing her ring-less fingers,
staring at the central display
a diamond and ruby wedding set.
She made no attempt
to wipe the tears spilling
from her memory.

I thought only of the gold buckle-ring
keeper token
given to my grandmother
in 1882
marking the intention of marriage.

This eternal circle symbol
entrusted to me
fell off my finger
last Sunday.

I heard echoes of my father's words
through my sobs
"Don't mourn worldly goods."
My mother's wails rise
from deep within
"You were entrusted with a family treasure."

On this bleak day
at yet another pawnshop,
my hopes for recovering

my gold buckle ring
diminish
as I also intently examine
the display.

THE FIELD

He recalls the general inspection
of the arena,
gags as the smell
fills his nostrils,
worming into his soul.

He picks his way through
the field of flesh.
Pauses,
hoping for signs of life.

"Even in a dung-heap,
a flower grows."
He once read.

His search for survivors continues.

A few feet away
a baby moves.

Do maggots have shoulders
on which to carry carrion?

THE TIP

"Don't ever complain of the smarting
when you bite your tongue.
You will have to tell
what lie caused it."
Was the tip my brother gave me.

I had to create an affair
with an older boy
with whom I shamelessly held hands
as we strolled in the park,
or kissed tight-lipped behind the blue-gum tree.
Only the forbidden would cause
lies of tongue-biting gravity.

The punishment was more bearable
than my mother's prodding
to get to the big lie.
Like a priest in the confessional
she expected a mortal sin.
My contrite sobbing also lessened
the punishment

with the tip of my tongue now aching,
I wish there could be an affair,
with a man far too young
for a woman of my age,
which would have warranted a tongue-biting.

FRIENDSHIP

in memory of Horace Bond

Friendship, like an oak,
grows roots deep
into the heart
of the earth.

It draws sustenance
and refreshment
from its place of planting.

Like the mighty oak
Friendship withstands
the winter chills
of adversity
and the steely grasps
of icy misunderstandings
piled on tender branches
which may break,
but allows the tree
hope for renewal
as spring coaxes
buds to new possibilities
of joy in bright green leaves
and flowers,
providing respite in its shade
from the heat
of disputes.

Friendship, like the wind

blowing fiercely or gently
through the summer leaves
creates music
of rhythms strong
pulsating
or gently soothing
in comfortable reassurances.

In the ever changing
seasons,
true friendship glories
in the splendor
of variety blazing
of autumn,
vivid reminders
of cycles,
ever constant
ever changing.
With roots deep and sure.

Friendship sturdy as the oak,
will remain in the heart
beyond time and space.

REKINDLING

She wanted to be content
inhaling the pine forest scent
from the low flickering candle.

In that room she recalled long walks
for berry-gathering in the Black Forest.

There where the sunlight shivered
through the branches
she enjoyed the quiet
far from the dance of bright lights.

As you wandered to the heart of the forest
in search of rare mushrooms,
she spent hours sitting on the dank ground
writing poems to be performed
in the glaring spotlights.

Now you have returned
to rekindle the fire in her soul,
to lead her away from the candles
which serve only as dim reminders
of the burning passion she once shared.

SEASON'S END

When the shy sun flirting
through the turning leaves
its cobweb pattern weaves,
I gather the last apples
for butter and cider stocks.

In this crisp freshness
free of stifling humidity,
the garden now at liberty
flaunts a wildness
in defiance of my training.

Enjoying this lemon sunlight
I do not lament summer's passing,
rather relish the quiet humming
backed by turtle-dove lullabies
before earth's long winter sleep.

THE LANGUAGE OF LIFE

Here my life is spoken
in the beeps of the machine
monitor of my rhythm
peeks spurting from valleys
beep beep beep.
For an hour or two
the sounds come to me
holding on to the now.
As if obeying the monotones
of a hypnotist
I fight to make sounds to words
that invite me to stay.
The sounds change.
Flatline
Buzzzzz.
I sink into blackness.
Code Blue. Code Blue.
The call is answered from all directions.
I float out of darkness
to shimmering brilliance
of a wide avenue
where my father and aunt promenade.
I shout an excited greeting,
run for reunion embrace,
but like a wader, my strides drag.
"Go back. Go back. It's not your time,"
my father warns.
I cannot reach them.
The body on the bed

draws me back.
Surrounded by green-capped heads.
Paddles. Clear.
I sink into darkness. Bounce back.
"She's back. Good rhythm."
Beep. Beep. Peaks and valleys.
The language of life resumes.

THE WALL

Walking in the mud
around St. Peter's, Chaldon
built 1065,
before the Conquest,
your wedding site,
I want to get inside
out of these sticky paths
to the Sanctuary.

You tell of Medieval paintings,
brasses, bells,
remember from school-girl visits,
days of your growing,
I missed.
After so many journeys
we traveled a narrow lane
in discomfort
air heavy with misgivings
unsaid memories.

At his place I need
your eyes disappearing
in joyous laughter, bubbling.
You, first-born daughter
of first-born daughter,
knew how to rejoice.

After forging your way
through narrow paths

to this place
we trudge through the mud
of the churchyard
filled with monuments,
large, small, imposing,
names and dates carried on the wind.

I am drawn to decipher
one small headstone
leaned against the wall
tossed away in a far corner.
"Suicide." You say. "Suicide." You repeat.
I had forgotten
those driven to the wall.

I wonder
what drives you relentlessly
to clash on the wall
with your mother.
I want to direct
you to the path
of forgiveness,
to the center, away from the wall.

Joy which should be here
before your wedding,
apology and forgiveness
are pathways from the wall.

EVENING AT FISH EAGLE

After the lilies have folded their petals,
and their stems stand tall
beside the floating leaves,
then darkness settles over the pond.

Tiny white reed frogs
take their places
where reflected stars are footlights
for individual lily pads.

When places are filled
in the concert hall,
the air trembles an overture.
The main feature begins
after tone and tune
is set by two leaders.
Soon the tiny reed frogs
swell to a song
which echoes from the hills.

In this majestic auditorium,
at the end of every song
the bull-frog croaks approval.

Printed in the United States
147988LV00003B/44/A